W9-AXS-792

What Others Say About Books & Programs by Andy Masters

"Andy Masters will add energy, content, and passion to your professional development event. Andy has the experiences and skills to keynote or conduct breakout sessions, including workshops and seminars. His content is fresh, relevant, and timely in every way imaginable. BOOK HIM for your next event."

- Wofford O'Sullivan, Conference Planner, after Andy's keynote program for 2,000+ attendees at the annual South Carolina Education and Business Summit

"Andy Masters' keynote captured the audience with his energy, approachability, and candor. The audience left not only inspired, but with techniques to achieve it. My only wish is that we would have had more time with him! FABULOUS way to conclude our great Conference!"

- Becky Musil, Associate Director, National Institute for Staff & Organizational Development (NISOD), after Andy's closing keynote for the 2013 NISOD Conference with 1,400+ attendees

"Andy did a GREAT job of integrating his trainings to ensure relevancy to National Hotel Association Executives. He was a SMASH HIT with the Association Executives attending the seminar. He integrates humor in such a way that everyone is engaged from beginning to end. I will DEFINITELY use Andy for future trainings!"

- Lisa Hamilton, President, Caribbean Society of Hotel Association Executives, after Andy's program with representatives from 12 countries in attendance

"Your presentation at both sessions was EXCELLENT – Entertaining and inspiring. It can be difficult holding the attention of fire chiefs but you engaged them and held their attention for the entire talk; both sessions. You used your own life experiences, laced with humor to get across a powerful life message that resonated with our attendees. I look forward to hearing more from you in the future and would certainly recommend you as a speaker to either public or private sector audiences. Thanks again and please stay in touch!"

- M. Stuart McElhaney, President, Florida Fire Chiefs Association (FFCA)

"Thank you so much for such a dynamic and effective presentation! I am still hearing very enthusiastic feedback from our chapter members about your talk, and wanted to tell you that for me personally, it has made a huge difference in my focus. I can't thank you enough for helping me see this!"

- Amy Erickson, Director of Professional Development, Rocky Mountain MPI

"Andy, you connected so well with our Young Business Professionals. You were energetic, motivating and down to Earth. You would be a huge asset to any group who is looking for an AMAZING, one-of-a-kind speaker!"

- Consuelo Inestrosa, Event Organizer, Young Business Professionals of Boca Raton

"The feedback I heard from yesterday was FANTASTIC and I thank you so much for coming. And most especially for dealing with all our last minute scheduling changes. You have been a pleasure to work with and I do hope we are able to bring you back for another visit!"

- Stephanie Moran, Network for Innovation and Leadership in Education, Sheridan Institute of Technology, Toronto, ON

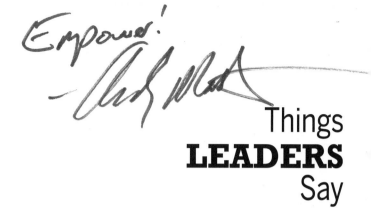

Things
LEADERS
Say

A Daily Guide to Help Every Leader
<u>Empower</u> & **<u>Inspire</u>**

Andy Masters

First Edition

Hawthorn Publishing
USA

Things LEADERS Say
A Daily Guide to Help Every Leader Empower & Inspire

By Andy Masters

Published by:
Hawthorn Publishing
U.S.A.

Printed in the United States of America

9 8 7 6

No part of this book may be reproduced or transmitted in any form or by any means, electronic or mechanical, including photocopying or by any information storage and retrieval system without written permission from the author, except for the inclusion of brief quotation in which quotation is fully attributed to the author.

Copyright © 2024 by Andy Masters
All rights reserved.

ISBN: 97809754610-1-3

Masters, Andy - 1st ed.

Acknowledgments

I'd like to thank the following contributors to this book:

Dave Clark, Lisa Crosby, Mark Dolitsky, Holly Duckworth, Scott Ginsberg, Steve Hughes, Joe Knecht, Matt Ronken, Renee Staggs, and Rick Strifler.

About The Author

Andy Masters is an award-winning author and international speaker who has presented hundreds of leadership, sales/service, and personal development programs.

He has written 5 books and earned 4 degrees, including an M.A. - Marketing and an M.A. - Human Resources Development from Webster University, as well as a B.A. - Communications and a B.A. - Political Science from the University of Missouri-St. Louis.

He has also been featured on many national media outlets, including <u>Leadership Excellence</u> magazine, <u>Investor's Business Daily</u>, and <u>LifeTime Television</u> network.

Andy has earned the prestigious "CSP" award/designation of the National Speakers Association (NSA), the highest earned international recognition for professional speakers, in which less than 10% of over 5,000+ speakers worldwide have achieved.

His website is www.Andy-Masters.com, and he can be contacted at Andy@Andy-Masters.com for speaking availability and volume book discounts for your event or organization.

Introduction

"An Easily Solvable Crisis"

We are in an era where managers are being asked to do more
with less, and wear multiple hats within every organization.
Business owners are drowning because of their obsession to
have a hand in all facets of the business, every day. Leaders at
all levels have never been more bogged-down and distracted
from incorporating true vision, implementing a plan, and
leading.

Enhancing the problem, initial promotions into management
are often given to the best "doer". The best salesperson is
promoted to sales manager. The best programmer is promoted
to IT manager. The best accountant is promoted to accounting
manager. These employees were GREAT at doing, but not prepared for LEADING. Further, when young managers are thrust
into a new leadership role, they are energetic to prove they can
handle it, are uncomfortable delegating, and attempt to "do-it-
all-themselves".

Either way, this workhorse mindset creates poor leadership
habits which persist for years—or even an entire career. It is
the way one becomes wired.

**"A leader isn't the person who takes on all responsibilities.
A leader is someone who empowers and inspires others to
achieve the goals of the organization as a team."**

Unfortunately, all of these factors lead to the mass production of overworked, stressed-out micro-managers and control freaks. This creates a chronic organizational culture of high stress, high burnout, high turnover, low quality, and low morale—with multiple levels of leadership who have an inability to truly lead. Organizations also realize needless costs for each hour a higher salaried manager does the work which could be done by a lower salaried employee—a terribly ineffective use of its human resources.

This is a crisis.

> *"Leaders who micro-manage spend more time looking down than looking up."*

There is a better way to lead.

We need to create an organizational culture in which leaders can see the forest through the trees. A culture where leaders understand the big picture of the organization, set high goals, and have tangible plans to achieve those goals. A culture where leaders are masters of developing, empowering, and delegating. A culture where leaders hire talented people, and provide them with the resources, support, coaching and inspiration to flourish.

Organizations MUST also provide training, development, and a future PLAN for each of those talented employees, and this plan must be supported 100% by each manager. This creates an upward distribution of responsibilities, where talented employees are encouraged to take on more, accelerating their development, while freeing up valuable time for the leader to focus on top objectives. This environment leads to higher morale, lower turnover, higher achievement, and improved succession planning.

People don't want to work for a dead-end job with repetitive, mundane responsibilities. This environment leads to high burnout, low morale, high turnover, and difficult succession planning.

People want to work for companies in which they have a future. People want to work for managers who believe in them. People want to feel valued, appreciated, and empowered.

Leaders create this environment through their actions and communications on a daily basis.

> *"Do your everyday actions and communications support your empowerment, and belief in your employees?"*

Today's leader needs to empower. Today's leader needs to inspire. Today's leader needs to foster a positive environment in which employees truly feel appreciated, and valued.

Today's leader is also quite busy, and needs daily reminders of such communications which empower and inspire.

Daily reminders of *Things LEADERS Say*.

Things
LEADERS
Say

Things **LEADERS** Say...

1.

"I appreciate your efforts. Why don't you take my parking spot next week?**"**

Andy Masters

Things **LEADERS** Don't Say...

1.

"If you work hard, someday you can get a parking spot like mine.**"**

Things **LEADERS** Say...

2.

"If we have to ruffle some feathers around here to make change happen, I'm ready.**"**

Things **LEADERS** Don't Say...

2.

"Hey, I don't want to ruffle any feathers around here."

Things **LEADERS** Say...

3.

"I've got your back.**"**

Things **LEADERS** Don't Say...

3.

"Don't make me look bad.**"**

Things **LEADERS** Say...

4.

"Folks, we're going to learn how to DANCE in the RAIN!"

Andy Masters

Things **LEADERS** Don't Say...

4.

"Things are tough out there. Just do the best you can and I hope we'll survive."

Things **LEADERS** Say...

5.

"Believe in me. I know this is the right direction for us."

Things **LEADERS** Don't Say...

5.

"What the heck, let's give this a shot."

Things **LEADERS** Say...

6.

"New rule: All meetings have a 30-minute time limit. Be on time. Be prepared. Make your points. Let's get it done."

Things **LEADERS** Don't Say...

6.

"I can't believe how many boring, unproductive meetings we have around here.**"**

Things **LEADERS** Say...

7.

"Here--I stopped by the store and picked up a new jar of Skittles for you. Awesome job yesterday."

Things **LEADERS** Don't Say...

7.

"Hey, do you have any more Skittles around? I love those things."

Things **LEADERS** Say...

8.

"Those gestures which truly build customer loyalty and employee loyalty are often no-cost or low-cost, and take little or no time."

Things **LEADERS** Don't Say...

8.

"We just don't have the time or budget around here for those sorts of things right now."

Things **LEADERS** Say...

9.

"The lifeblood of this company is treating every customer like royalty. LOVE your customer. Nothing is more important.**"**

Things **LEADERS** Don't Say...

9.

"I know customers can be a pain in the ass, but dealing with them is part of your job."

Things **LEADERS** Say...

10.

"Friday we're going to have an off-site retreat in a fun atmosphere for some team-building and creative brainstorming.**"**

Things **LEADERS** Don't Say...

10.

"I just placed an ideas suggestion box outside my office.**"**

Things **LEADERS** Say...

11.

"I will make sure you have the resources and training necessary to succeed in this position.**"**

Things **LEADERS** Don't Say...

11.

"Hey, I got thrown into the fire when I was in your position, too.**"**

Things **LEADERS** Say...

12.

"I know this has been on cruise control for a long time, but it's time to get creative and look for a better way.**"**

Things **LEADERS** Don't Say...

12.

"Hey, we've got this thing on cruise control. If it ain't broke, don't fix it.**"**

Things **LEADERS** Say...

13.

"I have tangible goals for us, and a tangible plan to achieve those goals.**"**

Things **LEADERS** Don't Say...

13.

"We'll get better….trust me.**"**

Things **LEADERS** Say...

14.

"Follow me, and we will set records."

Things **LEADERS** Don't Say...

14.

"My goal is just to keep things moving along this year."

Things **LEADERS** Say...

15.

"Tomorrow we will begin the process to re-write our mission statement. Everyone is encouraged to participate in its creation."

Things **LEADERS** Don't Say...

15.

"Here is our new mission statement which a consultant group helped the Board of Directors create."

Things **LEADERS** Say...

16.

"This investment in technology will allow us to be leaders in the industry over the next 10 years."

Things **LEADERS** Don't Say...

16.

"That's a lot of money to spend when what we've got works just fine.**"**

Things **LEADERS** Say...

17.

"I'm working on getting us help using other departments, temporary labor, and outsourcing some projects during this busy season.**"**

Things **LEADERS** Don't Say...

17.

"Hey, we're all swamped right now. Look at how many hours I worked last week!**"**

Things **LEADERS** Say...

18.

"I appreciate everyone staying late to get this done. I'll order pizza.**"**

Things **LEADERS** Don't Say...

18.

❝Try to hurry this up. All of the overtime charged against this project is killing me.❞

Things **LEADERS** Say...

19.

"Today we're going to brainstorm ideas to make this workplace FUN around here again. I truly want you to LOVE your job, and LOVE working here."

Things **LEADERS** Don't Say...

19.

"We don't have time for funny business around here. Now get to work.**"**

Things **LEADERS** Say...

20.

"Sales is everyone's job, and you represent your company each day. Who do you know that might need our products and services?**"**

Things **LEADERS** Don't Say...

20.

"Hey, that's Sales & Marketing's job, not ours."

Things **LEADERS** Say...

21.

"Cutting costs is everyone's job. What ideas do you have to save your company money, so that we can all benefit?**"**

Things **LEADERS** Don't Say...

21.

"Upper management is making us cut costs again."

Things **LEADERS** Say...

22.

"Today, we are unveiling a reward system to incentivize employees with ideas to enhance quality, improve processes, and cut costs.**"**

Things **LEADERS** Don't Say...

22.

"Things are so damn inefficient around here."

Things **LEADERS** Say...

23.

"I want to earn your respect.**"**

Andy Masters

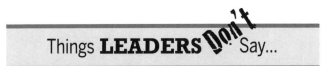

Things **LEADERS** Don't Say...

23.

"I'm in charge. I deserve respect.**"**

Things **LEADERS** Say...

24.

"I can't ignore this. What you did was wrong.**"**

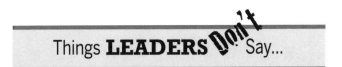

Things **LEADERS** Don't Say...

24.

"I'm going to pretend I didn't see that this time, and look the other way.**"**

Things **LEADERS** Say...

25.

"This issue is important to me. I will take action immediately.**"**

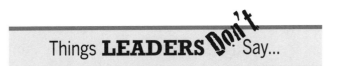

Things **LEADERS** Don't Say...

25.

"This issue is important to me. I'm going to create a task force which will make a recommendation 24 months from now on how to proceed.**"**

Things **LEADERS** Say...

26.

"I recognize that everyone on our team brings special talents and different backgrounds to the table. I hope you are as excited about that as I am. What an awesome team.**"**

Things **LEADERS** Don't Say...

26.

"Hey, we don't have to all like each other, but we have to at least tolerate each other."

Things **LEADERS** Say...

27.

"I'd like to give you some additional feedback today on how you're doing.**"**

Things **LEADERS** *Don't* Say...

27.

"Hey, performance reviews aren't for another 6 months.**"**

Things **LEADERS** Say...

28.

"There's a management position opening up in another department, and I'd like to recommend you.**"**

Things **LEADERS** Don't Say...

28.

"You're just too valuable to me in your current position to let you go.**"**

Things **LEADERS** Say...

29.

"To develop you from where you are right now, to where you want to be, this is the plan.**"**

Things **LEADERS** Don't Say...

29.

❝Trust me. There will be plenty of opportunities out there for you someday.❞

Things **LEADERS** Say...

30.

"We have a firm commitment to employee development.**"**

Things **LEADERS** Don't Say...

30.

"We have a firm commitment to employee development, as long as it doesn't cost any money, take time away from your job, or develop skills beyond what your current position requires."

Things **LEADERS** Say...

31.

"This week we will be implementing a comprehensive cross-training program, so we're prepared to cover for vacations, and handle any unexpected departures."

Things **LEADERS** Don't Say...

31.

"Two key employees just quit last week. Ummm…Does anyone know how to do their job?**"**

Things **LEADERS** Say...

32.

"I know this isn't a popular decision, but it's the right decision. I hope everyone can respect that.**"**

Things **LEADERS** Don't Say...

32.

"OK—You guys win."

Things **LEADERS** Say...

33.

"I understand there are some unpopular decisions coming down, but upper management is in a very difficult position right now.**"**

Things **LEADERS** Don't Say...

33.

"Upper management is really sticking it to us this time!**"**

Things **LEADERS** Say...

34.

"I know this is unpopular, but there are a few positives to this.**"**

Things **LEADERS** Don't Say...

34.

"I'm not happy about it either. This place SUCKS.**"**

Things **LEADERS** Say...

35.

"We want everyone's input on how to proceed."

Things **LEADERS** Don't Say...

35.

"Here's how we've decided to proceed. Any complaints?**"**

Things **LEADERS** Say...

36.

"Let's work together to brainstorm some cost-cutting solutions as a team."

Things **LEADERS** Don't Say...

36.

"As of July 1st, the following cost-cutting policies will be implemented."

Things **LEADERS** Say...

37.

"If anyone has suggestions on how we can do this better, I'm all ears.**"**

Things **LEADERS** Don't Say...

37.

"It's my way or the highway."

Things **LEADERS** Say...

38.

"I believe you are ready for this. Now is your time to shine.**"**

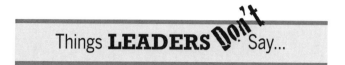

Things **LEADERS** Don't Say...

38.

"I'm not sure you're ready for this quite yet.**"**

Things **LEADERS** Say...

39.

"This is a very important project. I'd like to bring you along so you can contribute and develop.**"**

Things **LEADERS** Don't Say...

39.

"This is a very important project. I've got to tackle this one on my own."

Things **LEADERS** Say...

40.

"What are our options in this situation, and what do you recommend we do?**"**

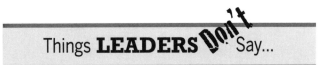

Things **LEADERS** Don't Say...

40.

"Put it on my desk and I'll figure it out later."

Things **LEADERS** Say...

41.

"That's a great idea…we should definitely consider it. Although, here's one impact that you might not have previously thought of.**"**

Things **LEADERS** Don't Say...

41.

"That's a bad idea, and here's why."

Things **LEADERS** Say...

42.

"Why are we having a busy, high-paid employee with expertise in a different skill set doing THIS?**"**

Things **LEADERS** Don't Say...

42.

"I don't care who is getting the work done, just as long as it's getting done.**"**

Things **LEADERS** Say...

43.

"I appreciate all of the extra hours you've been putting in lately. But over the long haul, you're too important for us to have you get burned out. How can I provide you with some help?**"**

Andy Masters

Things **LEADERS** Don't Say...

43.

"I love that you are working all hours of the night and weekends. That hard work and dedication is what we need more of around here!"

Things **LEADERS** Say...

44.

"Friday we're going to stop and celebrate the hard work and successes we've accomplished as a team. I've arranged for a surprise team event that will begin at 1:00."

Things **LEADERS** Don't Say...

44.

"Hey, we can't stop and celebrate now. There's plenty of hard work ahead of us."

Things **LEADERS** Say...

45.

"I've arranged for you to begin a job shadowing and cross-training program each week, as it will be great development for you in preparation for a future promotion."

Things **LEADERS** Don't Say...

45.

"We don't have time to do job shadowing and cross-training around here."

Things **LEADERS** Say...

46.

"You don't seem all that happy at work right now. What gives? Let's talk about it.**"**

Things **LEADERS** Don't Say...

46.

"Hey, if you don't want this job, I'll find someone who does.**"**

Things **LEADERS** Say...

47.

"I sincerely care about you and your challenges outside of work. Let me know how we can help.**"**

Things **LEADERS** Don't Say...

47.

"I don't care what's going on outside of work. You've got a job to do.**"**

Things **LEADERS** Say...

48.

"Let's talk about that project. What went well, what would you do differently, what did you learn?"

Things **LEADERS** Don't Say...

48.

"I'm really disappointed about your performance on that project. You've just GOT to do better next time."

Things **LEADERS** Say...

49.

"Unfortunately, performance reviews are only a one-way street. What would you like to see me do better, or do more of, for you?"

Things **LEADERS** Don't Say...

49.

"Hey, I'll worry about my performance—you worry about yours.**"**

Things **LEADERS** Say...

50.

"I trust you to get this done, and get it done right.**"**

Things **LEADERS** Don't Say...

50.

"If it's going to get done, and get done right, I might as well just do it myself.**"**

Things **LEADERS** Say...

51.

"I've hired a talented team and provided them with the resources and training necessary to succeed.**"**

Things **LEADERS** Don't Say...

51.

"I've been running around here doing everything myself for months!**"**

Things **LEADERS** Say...

52.

"Today is the day I must schedule two hours to work on my #1 project."

Things **LEADERS** Don't Say...

52.

"I can't believe I still haven't found time to work on my #1 project.**"**

Things **LEADERS** Say...

53.

"My number one priority each day is to be sure we're on exact course to reach our goals."

Things **LEADERS** Don't Say...

53.

"I spend so much time in the trenches I can't even remember what our goals were.**"**

Things **LEADERS** Say...

54.

"If I'm the only one who knows how to do this, I can't ever enjoy a vacation—and I'm squelching the development of others who really need to learn and advance.**"**

Things **LEADERS** Don't Say...

54.

"If I'm the only one who knows how to do this, they can't fire me. And if they do, they will be screwed!**"**

Things **LEADERS** Say...

55.

"I'm leaving on vacation for 2 weeks, and won't be checking email or voice mail. You're in charge now. I trust you.**"**

Things **LEADERS** *Don't* Say...

55.

"I'm leaving on vacation for 2 weeks. Call my cell anytime day or night and I'll be checking email constantly."

Things **LEADERS** Say...

56.

"I appreciate you jumping in to take action when management wasn't available.**"**

Things **LEADERS** Don't Say...

56.

"Who died and made YOU King?"

Things **LEADERS** Say...

57.

"I try to take on a leadership mindset with everything I do.**"**

Things **LEADERS** Don't Say...

57.

"I don't have any employees, so I'm not a leader.**"**

Things **LEADERS** Say...

58.

"I'm giving you more responsibility because I believe in you.**"**

Andy Masters

Things **LEADERS** Don't Say...

58.

"Someday you'll be ready for more responsibility."

Things **LEADERS** Say...

59.

"I want to do everything we can to maximize your talents and abilities around here.**"**

Things **LEADERS** Don't Say...

59.

"I understand that you might be great at some other things, but that's not your job here.**"**

Things **LEADERS** Say...

60.

"You're doing great. Let's work together to make you the BEST at what you do, because I believe you can be the best."

Things **LEADERS** Don't Say...

60.

"You're doing great...I don't have to pay attention to you at all!"

Things **LEADERS** Say...

61.

"You know what needs to be done, and you have the resources to do it. So go make it great.**"**

Things **LEADERS** Don't Say...

61.

"Do it this way."

Things **LEADERS** Say...

62.

"If you run into any roadblocks, let me know and I'll get involved right away.**"**

Things **LEADERS** Don't Say...

62.

"If you run into any roadblocks, just plow through 'em!"

Things **LEADERS** Say...

63.

"Next Monday I want to share with everyone ideas from the conference I'm attending this weekend, and brainstorm action steps to implement those ideas.**"**

Things **LEADERS** Don't Say...

63.

"I'm headed to our annual conference this weekend in Las Vegas, baby…Cha-Ching!!**"**

Things **LEADERS** Say...

64.

"I'd like for you to get more involved with our industry association, such as contributing to the blog and attending this year's conference. It will be great for your development.**"**

Things **LEADERS** Don't Say...

64.

"I'll bring you back some notes from my conference.**"**

Things **LEADERS** Say...

65.

"I wouldn't offer you this project if I didn't think you could handle it. This is a great opportunity for you to show everyone your talents—and I know you will.**"**

Things **LEADERS** Don't Say...

65.

"If you can't handle this project, I'll give it to someone else who can.**"**

Things **LEADERS** Say...

66.

"I hired you because I believe that you can transform this position into something special.**"**

Things **LEADERS** Don't Say...

66.

"Just try to keep the ball rolling."

Things **LEADERS** Say...

67.

"This is one area that's not a strength of mine. That's why I hired you. I trust you."

Things **LEADERS** Don't Say...

67.

"I take pride in being a jack-of-all-trades.**"**

Things **LEADERS** Say...

68.

"Congratulations on your promotion. I'm 100% confident you are going to accomplish incredible things with this new opportunity."

Things **LEADERS** Don't Say...

68.

"OK, I finally gave you this promotion. Now don't screw it up.**"**

Things **LEADERS** Say...

69.

"I want to listen to you.**"**

Things **LEADERS** Don't Say...

69.

"Listen to me.**"**

Things **LEADERS** Say...

70.

"I'd like to know what you think.**"**

Things **LEADERS** Don't Say...

70.

"I don't pay you to think."

Things **LEADERS** Say...

71.

"I would love to hear your ideas on how the department can improve.**"**

Things **LEADERS** Don't Say...

71.

"This is the way we have always done it, and there is no reason to change. Focus on your own responsibility and I'll focus on the department."

Things **LEADERS** Say...

72.

"Here's why we need to do this.**"**

Andy Masters

Things **LEADERS** Don't Say...

72.

"Just do it."

Things **LEADERS** Say...

73.

"I understand you have some valid complaints. Let me see what I can do to help.**"**

Things **LEADERS** Don't Say...

73.

"You think YOU have it bad? Look at my job!"

Things **LEADERS** Say...

74.

"My door is always open. Bring me the good, the bad, and the ugly."

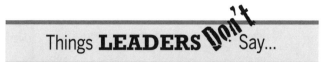

Things **LEADERS** Don't Say...

74.

"Don't come to me with your problems."

Things **LEADERS** Say...

75.

"First and foremost, I care about you and your well-being.**"**

Things **LEADERS** Don't Say...

75.

"Hey, you've got a job to do, so just do it."

Things **LEADERS** Say...

76.

"It's important to me that you enjoy your job, and enjoy working here. How can I help?**"**

Things **LEADERS** *Don't* Say...

76.

"You should feel lucky to just have a job right now.**"**

Things **LEADERS** Say...

77.

"How can I help you?"

Things **LEADERS** Don't Say...

77.

"How can you help me?"

Things **LEADERS** Say...

78.

"Do as I do.**"**

Andy Masters

Things **LEADERS** Don't Say...

78.

"Do as I say, not as I do."

Things **LEADERS** Say...

79.

"Even though I'm in charge, it's important for me that I have your respect.**"**

Things **LEADERS** Don't Say...

79.

"I don't care if you respect me or not, I'm in charge.**"**

Things **LEADERS** Say...

80.

"I understand that you are super-busy right now. Based on your schedule, when do you think you can get this project done by?**"**

Things **LEADERS** Don't Say...

80.

"I need this done by this Friday.**"**

Things **LEADERS** Say...

81.

"I know you're busy, but time is of the essence if you could help right away.**"**

Things **LEADERS** Don't Say...

81.

"Drop everything and get in here NOW."

Things **LEADERS** Say...

82.

"I appreciate your extra efforts during this tough period. But there is a light at the end of the tunnel.**"**

Things **LEADERS** Don't Say...

82.

"Hey, it's tough on everyone around here these days.**"**

Things **LEADERS** Say...

83.

"You work with me, not for me.**"**

Things **LEADERS** Don't Say...

83.

"You work for me.**"**

Things **LEADERS** Say...

84.

"I want to make you look good.**"**

Things **LEADERS** Don't Say...

84.

"Make me look good."

Things **LEADERS** Say...

85.

"Complain not. Other departments have their challenges, too. We are only strong if we get along.**"**

Things **LEADERS** Don't Say...

85.

"We can't do our job if other departments keep screwing us up."

Things **LEADERS** Say...

86.

"It doesn't matter whose fault it is. Let's work through it to find a solution.**"**

Things **LEADERS** Don't Say...

86.

"It was their fault.**"**

Things **LEADERS** Say...

87.

"That was my fault."

Things **LEADERS** Don't Say...

87.

"That was your fault."

Things **LEADERS** Say...

88.

"We screwed up."

Things **LEADERS** Don't Say...

88.

"One of my employees screwed up.**"**

Things **LEADERS** Say...

89.

"Don't worry about making mistakes. Push the boundaries, take chances, and learn from your mistakes along the way."

Things **LEADERS** Don't Say...

89.

"Don't make any mistakes."

Things **LEADERS** Say...

90.

"Here is the contingency plan we should all be familiar with. It's now time to put this in motion. Let's get moving."

Things **LEADERS** Don't Say...

90.

"About ten years ago, I think we came up with a contingency plan for our ISO certification. It should be in some file cabinet somewhere."

Things **LEADERS** Say...

91.

"I'm concerned that if this trend persists, we are going to have a major problem on our hands. What can we do *now*?**"**

Things **LEADERS** *Don't* Say...

91.

"Hey, if this gets worse, I'll worry about it then.**"**

Things **LEADERS** Say...

92.

"We've got a number of challenges right now which I know we will eventually overcome.**"**

Things **LEADERS** Don't Say...

92.

"We're screwed."

Things **LEADERS** Say...

93.

"We have to notify our client of this."

Things **LEADERS** Don't Say...

93.

"What they don't know won't hurt 'em."

Things **LEADERS** Say...

94

"I know this seems bad, but mistakes are simply opportunities to strengthen relationships. How can we respond so that our client actually *gains* respect for us?**"**

Andy Masters

Things **LEADERS** Don't Say...

94.

"We did WHAT!?!!!!?!?? #%#& !!!!!!!!!!!!!!!!!!!!!!"

Things **LEADERS** Say...

95.

"Everyone stay calm. I'll get on the phone and handle some type of resolution."

Things **LEADERS** Don't Say...

95.

"AAAAAAAAAAAAAAHHHHHHHHHHHHHHHHH!!!!!!!!!!!"

Things **LEADERS** Say...

96.

"I appreciate this award. It's been a privilege to be a part of this team. They are the ones who deserve this award.**"**

Things **LEADERS** Don't Say...

96.

"I appreciate this award. I've tried hard to get the most out of this group under the circumstances, and I've had to overcome a lot of challenges."

Things **LEADERS** Say...

97.

"My department is doing the best they can under the circumstances. I'm proud of their efforts."

Things **LEADERS** Don't Say...

97.

"My department is killing me. I need more people, and better people, to accomplish anything.**"**

Things **LEADERS** Say...

98.

"Even though we won't be working together anymore, always know you can call on me for help or advice."

Things **LEADERS** Don't Say...

98.

"Good luck....See you around!"

Things **LEADERS** Say...

99.

"I hope you've all grown from our time together. I know I have. And I know you all will take this organization to new heights after I leave.**"**

Things **LEADERS** Don't Say...

99.

"This place is going to fall apart after I leave."

Things **LEADERS** Say...

100.

"You did it.**"**

Things **LEADERS** Don't Say...

100.

" I did it. **"**

Things **LEADERS** Say...

101.

"Thank you.**"**

Things **LEADERS** Don't Say...

101.

Contact Andy

For more information
about Andy's award-winning
books and programs,
please visit:

www.Andy-Masters.com